I Recall Nothing

Sadie Laporte

BookLeaf
Publishing

Presentation by BookLeaf Publishing

Web: www.bookleafpub.com

E-mail: info@bookleafpub.com

ISBN: 9789357612371

First edition 2022

DEDICATION

This book is for James,

Thank you for always answering your phone,

with love

Safe House

It's quiet tonight.
I tell myself I am safe here.
Up high.
Doors locked, curtains drawn.
There is stillness.
There is calm.
I look around at the space I've created.
Soft blankets thrown on the sofa, art and pictures
adorn the walls.
Books and music strategically placed on the
shelf.
I get a sense of stability.
A sense of home.
A candle lights the backdrop to my world.
A world where there is no yelling.
No monsters walking the halls.
No needles on the bathroom floor.
No cocaine scattered like powdered sugar across
the coffee table.
My things aren't getting
stolen,
broken.
I'm safe here.
Up high.

This place is nothing to no one but everything to
me.
In every room, behind every corner, I see life,
love,
home.
If peace is a river let it wash over me.
As I sit in my Safe House.
Under a birch tree,
Up high.

Of Monsters & Men

I never asked my mother to check my room for
the boogeyman,
I was never that naive.
Because I knew he slept a few feet down the
hall,
one fell swoop,
and he would be out to get me.

Dial Tones

Dial Tones
I'm not sure what to call you,
"Mom" doesn't sound quite right.
Your name, too impersonal.
So I don't call at all.
I leave the phone off the hook.
Just another night,
where all we share are dial tones.

I'm wide awake, It's morning

I asked Father Time why he doesn't change the
wiring of my brain to sleep.
He said clock hands can't move for the girl
hiding under bed sheets.
Insomnia they call it.
A pattern of sleeplessness.
A problem to those who need to rise before
dawn.
I've faked a lot of things in life,
but never a yawn.
I rush through the evening routine.
Wash, brush, repeat.
Staring at the hollowed-out eyes of a girl who
doesn't know how to chase dreams.
How can I chase dreams when dreaming
requires sleeping, and sleeping requires you to
shut off?
Unlike a toy, there is no button for that.
I guess that's where daydreaming comes into
play.
There is no rest for the wicked they have told
me.

I guess wicked is a title that has somehow come
to own me.
I wrote to The Sandman asking for some sleep in
my eyes.
I haven't yet heard.
Can't say I'm surprised.

The Quiet Things That No One Ever Knows

Purple patches left on porcelain skin remind me
that this isn't what love looks like.
This is malicious,
vicious,
cruel.
This is hurt.
This is pain.
Purple patches left on porcelain skin remind me
that I have been thrown,
cast aside like yesterday's news.
My head has hit walls as hard as the heart of the
man who threw me.
Frantic.
Scramble.
Panic.
Seeing lights explode like fireworks from the
hidden places of my brain.
Don't cry little girl,
tears leave a stain.
Carefully placed clothing.

Layer up.
School in the morning.
Hush now don't say a word.
Purple patches left on porcelain skin remind me
that hands have wrapped themselves around
wrists that protested.
Restrained to nights locked out of my own room.
Purple patches left on porcelain skin,
have now...
Faded.

It's Alright Ma I'm Only Burning

You say I don't know the hell that you've walked through.
I am here to tell you that you dragged me right along behind you.
As the flames licked my skin, you shielded your eyes and didn't look back to see just how badly I was burned.

We Might As Well Be Strangers

You never taught me how to braid my hair.
As I fight with the knotted ends, twisting and
pulling the pieces trying to get them to form
something,
Form anything.
You never taught me how to braid my hair.
We saw each other today, stopped at the red light
in town.
We gestured, like two people who used to know
one another.
As I turned the corner my only thought was,
"Where did you get the bicycle?"

Bare Bones

My skeletons don't hide in the closet,
They are out walking the streets around town.
My skeletons aren't bags of bones.
But they appear as one.
My skeletons are the "junkies"
The "come help me's"
The " save me's"
My skeletons are lost,
but not forgotten.

Bandages

I'm scraping the bottom of the barrel it seems,
collecting scraps.
I've been using Band-Aids for wounds that are
more than surface deep.
Hoping that this time,
I won't come apart at the seams.

Like You Like an Arsonist

I've been dragging my hands over the coals that
you burned in me when I was five years old.
Trying to get warm from the ashes of what could
have been,
What never was,
And what was meant to be.
Cold homes don't produce warmth.
You act as though I've pushed you away,
When you never tried to hold me close in the
first place.

Frigid

When the cold comes sweeping, in my mind
I'm thinking.
That you have nowhere to go.
Wandering the streets around town,
A gypsy soul, without a home.

Mother's Helper

Our eyes may look alike but we don't see the
same way.
I was just a child, taught to shoulder weight that
wasn't mine to carry.
You are the definition of arbitrary.

Come Find Me

Look for me in the valley of chaos.
Playing along the riverbanks of self doubt, and
insecurities.
Look for me.
Shine a light.
Start a fire.
Lost among the hydrangeas.
Sitting on legs that refuse to walk by faith.
Heavy, from the weight of my sins.
I don't remember how I ended up here.
Come find me.
I forget where home is.
Come find me.
Show me what love is.

Let me in, I'm outside

Little fists pound themselves on locked doors to childhood dreams.
Little fists clenched to things unseen.

The Tide That Left And Never Came Back

You abandoned ship before it ever started
sinking.
You used me as a life raft.
A buoy to hold you afloat.
And when the tide came in,
you hit the shore.
While I floated out.

Slow Dancing

I've romanticized what I thought grief would feel
like,
smell like, taste like.
What I thought it would be like, to "get over" as
if Grief could possibly be chalked up to a series
of events that you someday let go of.
That I know of,
You can't rationalize Grief.
I dressed her up in pretty words, sprinkled her
with fairy dust and blew her away.
She didn't get very far.
She doesn't like to be peeled back,
stripped down,
bare-boned.
You can't hide from her
run from her,
drown her.
Someday you might want to face her.
I can promise you, she won't be easy.
She dances in with the night.
Sneaks up on you,
uninvited,
unnerving
unwarranted
unmerciful.

Truthfully she doesn't know any other way to be.

20

Unsteady

3 a.m isn't for the happy people asleep in their bed.
3 a.m is for the survivors, trying to get a glimpse of what living looks like.

Home Improvement

I've been building my fortress of solitude for years.
Using depression as the foundation.
Anxiety nailed to the walls.
Insecurities mark up the floorboards,
down the hallway to the panic room.
Jodie Foster doesn't live here.
Peeking out only when the rest of the world has succumbed to slumber.
Don't let anyone in.
And don't you dare...let yourself out.

Let's Go Living

With eyes as round as dinner plates,
 and cheeks that fold like crepes.
She smells of neglect & cigarettes
I don't want to believe this could be her fate.

It's okay to think about ending

She lay broken,
In a thousand pieces on the floor.
Life no more.
Her adult life is an endless black hole full of
madness.
And when she closes her eyes she sees only
sadness.
She doesn't know how it hurts her family so,
To see her lying on the ground.
Cold as snow.

…

I penned those words at fourteen.
I want to go back and write it over.
Scratch it out.
Make you sober.
Our parting words were worse than those
rhymes.
I saddled you with guilt,
And this time it's all mine.

Please forgive me for my lack of gumption,
I shouldn't have made the assumption.
I went back to the last second before we ended
our call.
I should have noticed the tone,
The plea,
The fall.

An ending no one wants to hear
You gave me life.
Mom,
have you really been gone half a year?

The search for something more

In the end, I learned that it was okay to vomit up dozens of pages stained with blood and smeared ink.
It meant I had something to say.
It meant that the fragments, blurred lines, and all of the mess I was holding in had a place to go.

Book description:

You're holding the bits.
Collected thoughts over spilled cups of coffee.
When the sun took a bow, and the moon entered
centre stage.
Here they come…
 The wounds,
The mending,
Alive.